RELEASE

A 14 Day Devotional

Overcome Emotional Wounds and Live the Life You Were Created to Live

By

Mithra Woods Bell

This book is dedicated to my grandmothers, Earline P. Walker and Edna Mae Woods; for their love and support. My grandmothers were such great examples of what it meant to be a strong woman and a woman of faith. Most of all, I thank them for introducing me to the Lord.

To my wonderful guy, Anthony J. Bell Sr. I love you. I am grateful to have such a loving, supportive life partner. I thank God daily for you. Thank you for accepting and loving me, just as I am.

To my children, Charreka, Anthony Jr., and Aaron. Your mom is so incredibly proud of each of you. God has so much in store for you all. To my grandbabies, Shy'rion, and Antione. Mimi loves you. Always remember, God loves you most.

I pray this book will help bring healing to those of you, who like me, are in the fight to overcome the emotional wounds that left us struggling with insecurity, self-confidence, low self-esteem and acceptance. God loves you and He accepts you. God's love is real, and it will heal you if you allow it to.

Table of Contents

Introduction 1

Day 1   Believe and Receive 3

Day 2   Healing for Your Heart 5

Day 3   Be Free 7

Day 4   Handpicked and Chosen 9

Day 5   You Are Accepted 11

Day 6   Opinions are Opinions 13

Day 7   What Are You Talking About? 15

Day 8   Gather Your Thoughts 17

Day 9   Ohh, So Loved 19

Day 10   Tell Him All About It 21

Day 11   Forgiveness is Key 23

Day 12   Brand New 25

Day 13   The Exchange 27

Day 14   Release. Let Go. 29

INTRODUCTION

At first glance, most of us appear to have our lives in order. We may have a wonderful job, money in the bank, a great spouse and well-behaved, intelligent children. On the surface, things appear to be all put together neat and tidy; however, when examined more closely, many of us are an emotional wreck.

We have unhealed emotional wounds that are secretly affecting all areas of our lives. Unlike physical wounds, emotional wounds are very easy to conceal. Some of us have become so good at hiding the emotional wounds that we fool ourselves not realizing that we are hurting, ultimately causing harm to ourselves. Many of us have become so accustomed to the emotional scars of past traumas that we just push through life pretending that these scars do not exist.

The thing is, they are still there. As a social worker, I see many adults who are living fractured and unhappy lives due to emotional scars that they never properly dealt with so that they can heal. As a result, they have become "infected". If left untreated, this infection starts to spill over and poison the entire life.

The good news is God sees our emotional wounds and He is ready and able to help us overcome the emotional pain and set us on the path to healing so that we can break free and live the life He created us to live.

DAY 1

BELIEVE AND RECEIVE

"If you openly declare that Jesus is Lord and believe in your heart that God raised Him from the dead, you will be saved."

Romans 10:9 NLT

True healing can only be received by, and through faith in Jesus. In order to start the healing process, you must believe the Lord is who He says He is. If you have not already accepted Him as your Lord and Savior, now is a great time to do so.

If you have already received Jesus, renew your commitment to Him and ask Him to help you overcome and heal from the emotional wounds left by past traumas.

Your ability to live as the person God created you to be is directly linked to your relationship with Him. True healing can only come through the Lord. He loves you. He wants a personal relationship with you. Give Him your burdens and hurts. Depend on Him completely for your healing and you will be healed.

3

The journey to healing will not be easy. You may feel that you can't be healed because you have lived with the pain for so long; or maybe it's too much. Know that God will be with you every step of the way. God is not only concerned about your eternity; He also cares about your life here on Earth. You can be whole and happy. You can be healed.

Say this: Dear God, I come to you just as I am, wounded and broken. I accept your Son, Jesus Christ as Lord and Savior. I believe He died for me and was raised from the dead. I ask you to forgive me and save me. Lord, break the bondage of the emotional wounds in my life. I believe I can live the life you created me to live. I commit my life to you and I receive your complete healing in my life. Thank you for loving and caring for me. Amen.

Day 2

Healing for Your Heart

"The Lord is close to the brokenhearted;
he rescues those whose spirits are crushed."

Psalm 34:18 NLT

I used to think that God was this big invisible Being, seated way up in heaven waiting for me to mess up so that He could punish me for breaking His rules. The truth is, God is not far away from us. He is a loving caring Father who is near to us. He is concerned with every aspect of our lives.

He desires **you** to be whole in every area of your life. God wants to heal you. He is deeply concerned about the hurt that has left you wounded.

God promises to never leave or forsake His children. God's power is made strong in our weakness. He wants to rescue us from the painful trauma. You can depend on Him totally for your healing.

God also promises healing to His children; however, the promises of God are not automatic. You must believe He is and that He keeps every promise. Then by, you must receive and take possession, of the healing God has for you.

Say this: God is close to me. He loves me and is concerned for me. He offers me complete healing. Today I choose to accept God's love and healing for my brokenness.

DAY 3

BE FREE

"Therefore, if the Son sets you free, you shall be free indeed."

John 8:36 NKJV

The Bible tells us that in Jesus we have peace, joy and victory. This is what we are entitled to as children of the King. Unfortunately, many of us are not experiencing any of the promises that come with salvation. It is an unfortunate truth that some of us are not experiencing any joy, peace or victory in our lives. We are still bound although we have been set free, either because we do not know, do not believe, or have not accepted it.

God offers us salvation when we accept His Son as our Savior but this is not the end. We also are promised an abundant life full of peace, joy, acceptance, and freedom. However, we must open our heart to receive the gifts of God. Remember, His promises are received by faith.

While the life of a Christian is not perfect, we all have trials we must go through. God promises to be with us through the midst of it all and at the end it will work out for our good.

Say this: Jesus has set me free. I am indeed free. I will no longer walk in bondage. I will live in my God-given freedom. This freedom allows me to live with peace, joy and love.

Handpicked and Chosen

"Even before He made the world. God loved us and chose us in Christ to be holy and without fault in Him."

Ephesians 1:4 NLT

Growing up, we used to sing a little song that said, "sticks and stones may break my bones but words will never hurt me". As cute as this may sound, the truth is words do hurt. For some of us, we were hurt by the words hurled at us from those who were closest to us. You may have been told that you were a mistake. Perhaps you were harshly criticized or ostracized. Maybe you were told you would never amount to anything, or called stupid or worthless.

Words can cut deeply leaving lifelong scars and destructive impacts. Mental health experts agree; if left unresolved, childhood traumas can have a profound affect reaching into adulthood. These types of wounds greatly affect emotional development, in many cases causing low self-esteem, the ability to recognize and maintain healthy relationships and much more.

Know this, you are not a mistake. God planned your existence. The time, date and location of your birth were all intentional. The circumstances surrounding your conception does not matter. Despite what others may have said to you, you are not a mistake. You were chosen by God and He has a plan for your life. God chose you before He laid the foundation of the earth. He loved you even then. God chose you as His own. Others may have rejected you, but God chose you. It does not matter what others say or think about you. What matters is what God says about you. He is your creator, and His thoughts toward you are good.

Say this. I have been chosen by God. He has a plan for my life. I am not a mistake. God planned for my existence before the foundation of the earth was laid. Today, I believe I am chosen by God for His good work. My worth and identity are determined by God.

YOU ARE ACCEPTED

"Although my father and my mother have abandoned me, Yet the Lord will take me up [adopt me as His child]."

Psalm 27:10 AMP

Have you ever felt like you did not belong? Have you ever felt unaccepted, unloved or rejected? I have. I know many of you have as well. We all have an innate desire to belong. We all want to feel accepted and wanted. When children do not feel accepted and loved it can affect them well into adulthood.

Abandonment and rejection can be life altering. This can hurt deeply, leaving one stuck in the belief that they are unworthy and unwanted, especially when it comes from the ones who we expect to love us most, family. It affects the way we see ourselves, the way we interact with others and the way we live in the world.

Although you may have been rejected or abandoned by others, God calls you His own. While others may have rejected you,

God says you are wanted and accepted. God has validated you and put His stamp of approval of you. God loves you with an everlasting love. God calls you His beloved. You are God's beloved (I John 3:2). Nothing can stop God from loving you. He will never change His mind about you. He will never leave you or forsake you.

Say this: God accepts me just as I am. He loves me with an everlasting love. He will never abandon me. In God I am valuable, worthy and good enough.

DAY 6

OPINIONS ARE OPINIONS

"The fear of human opinion disables;
Trusting in God protects you from that."

Proverbs 29:25 MSG

Let's face it, everyone has an opinion. Opinions are not an issue, as long as they are seen for what they are; a person's view on something or someone. Opinions are rarely based on facts or knowledge. They are just about what that person perceives about something or someone.

As harmless as opinions appear, other people's opinions become problematic when we allow them to interfere with, and control our life. Trying to please people will quickly break you. People are fickle. One day they are with you, the next day they are not. Do not live for the approval of people; rather live your life for God. He already loves you, accepts you and sees you for who you truly are.

God is our creator and what He says about us is the truth based on what He knows about His creation. Free yourself from the opinions and approval of people and trust what God says.

Say this: I am free from people's opinions of me. I will no longer seek to please people but I will only seek to please God. God loves and accepts me as is.

WHAT ARE YOU TALKING ABOUT?

"For assuredly, I say to you, whoever says to this mountain, 'Be removed and be cast into the sea,' and does not doubt in his heart, but believes that those things he says will be done, he will have whatever he says."

Mark 11:23 NKJV

Tell me, what do you say about yourself? I used to be so negative about myself. If someone paid me a compliment, I would point out something wrong with me. Someone would say, "I like your outfit". I would say something like, "it does not fit right; it would be cuter on you".

Frequently, those of us with emotional wounds have very low opinions of ourselves. We believe that we are defective in some way. This often manifests as negative self-talk which could be internal or verbalized. Both are damaging.

15

The Bible says life and death are in the power of the tongue. Do you speak life or death to yourself? God created you, and you are marvelous in His eyes. You are who God says you are. Say and believe what God says about you. You will have the life you talk about.

Say this: I will say about myself what God says about me. I am fearfully and wonderfully made. I am not inferior to anyone. I am who God says I am and I will live the life He says I can have.

GATHER YOUR THOUGHTS

"And now, dear brothers and sisters, one final thing. Fix your thoughts on what is true, and honorable, and right, and pure, and lovely, and admirable. Think about things that are excellent and worthy of praise."

Romans 4:8 NLT

What you say and what you think go hand and hand. Thoughts become words. When you have been abandoned or rejected by someone the wound cuts deep. You may ask yourself, "What's wrong with me?" "Why don't they want me?" You may start to believe there is something defective about you.

In order to heal, it is imperative to change the way you think, especially about yourself. The Apostle Paul tells us in Philippians to fix our thoughts on what is true and honorable, right and pure. What is true is that you are God's beloved. He loves you and to Him you are beautiful and wonderfully made. God is so into you He knows how many hairs are on your head.

Having negative thoughts about yourself only inflicts more emotional wounds on you. It is self-torture. We all have moments where we do not feel or think the best about ourselves. The key is to not ponder on these thoughts. Counter the negative thoughts with the pure truth.

Say this: I will manage my thought life. I will think on things that edify me not tear me down.

OHH, SO LOVED

"For God so loved the world that He gave His only begotten Son, that whoever believes in Him should not perish but have everlasting life."

John 3:16 NLT

What are you willing to pay for something that you love and deem valuable? God considered you so valuable that He gave up His beloved Son's life for yours.

Even though I grew up in church, I never knew that God loved me until I was an adult. I am not sure why I didn't know, but I did not know. Once I learned and accepted this wonderful truth my life changed forever.

God loves you and He demonstrated that love by sending Jesus to save you and give you an abundant life. Even today, He still shows His love by being active in the life of believers. You are loved and are valuable to the Creator of the entire universe. Think about that for a moment. YOU are loved by

God. God loves you. I really want you to grasp this, believe this, and live like it is true because it is.

Say this: God loves me with an unfailing, everlasting love. His love for me will never change. I am loved by God.

DAY 10

TELL HIM ALL ABOUT IT

"Cast all your cares (all your anxieties, all your worries, and all your concerns, once and for all) on Him, for He cares about you (with deepest affection, and watches over you very carefully)."

I Peter 5:7 AMP

Some of the by-products of emotional wounds are fear, worry and anxiety. We who have been emotionally wounded tend to worry about things like, "Do they like me?" "What do they think about me?" "What if I can't?" "What if this doesn't work?" We have anxiety about the what ifs and we are fearful to live life because we don't want to be wounded any further. This is not the life that God has planned for you.

A life full of worry, anxiety and fear is opposite of the life God has for us. He wants our life to be filled with joy, peace and love.

The life of a Christian is not free from troubles; however, we can rejoice in knowing that God is there to help us get through the ups and downs in life. No matter what difficulties we face God wants us to give Him all of it. All of your wounds, worries, anxieties and concerns, give them to God. After you have turned them over to Him, leave them there no matter how tempting it may be to pick them back up. Allow God to handle these things for you.

Say this: God I am casting all my cares, anxieties, worries and wounds on You. I totally depend on You to take care of me. I know You love me and you watch over all things concerning me.

FORGIVENESS IS KEY

"If you forgive those who sin against you, your heavenly Father will forgive you."

Matthew 6:14 NLT

When someone hurts you, a wide range of emotions are created: anger, sadness, surprise and rage are a few. You want to know why this person hurt you. You ask yourself, "How could they betray me like this? "Often, we want to immediately cut them out of our lives or seek revenge or both. However, this is not how God wants us to handle those who have hurt us. Because God has forgiven us, he expects us to forgive others.

No, forgiving someone that hurt you will not be easy. It may even seem irrational and unnatural to do so but it's what God requires us to do and He will give us the grace to do so. Forgiving a person is not only beneficial to that person; it helps you as well. Forgiving the person that hurt you sets you free. My grandmother would often say unforgiveness is like a cancer that spreads until your whole soul is poisoned.

Forgive that you may be forgiven. Forgive in order to protect your peace. Forgive because God requires it.

Say this: God, please help me to forgive those who have hurt me, completely, totally and permanently.

DAY 12

BRAND NEW

"Therefore, if anyone is in Christ {that is, grafted in, joined to Him by faith as savior}, he is a new creature [reborn and renewed by the Holy Spirit]; the old things [the previous moral and spiritual condition] have passed away. Behold, new things have come [because spiritual awakening brings a new life]."

2 Corinthians 5:17 AMP

When I was young I had very low self-esteem. This was a result of many different factors but the point is I did not view myself in a positive light. After I received Jesus into my life and began to learn about how He sees me and who I am in Him, my view of myself changed. This did not happen overnight, of course, but over time I developed more confidence, not in myself, but in who I am in Him. The scripture says, "When you are in Christ you become new". Another translation says "Anyone united in Christ gets a fresh start, is created new." In Christ, you take on a new nature and this causes your view of things to also be new. Not only is the sinful nature gone but your poor view of yourself is transformed. You are even able to see those that hurt you in a different light. It is only in and through Christ that we can know our identity. When you are in Him you get to learn who you truly are. Throw off those old labels put on you by yourself and others. They are gone; they have passed away. Receive your new identity in Christ.

Say this: I am in Christ; therefore, I am a new creation. Old things have passed away. I choose to accept my identity in Christ.

THE EXCHANGE

"To all who mourn in Israel, He will give a crown of beauty for ashes, a joyous blessing instead of mourning, festive praise instead of despair. In their righteousness, they will be like great oaks that the Lord has planted for His own glory."

Isaiah 61:3 NLT

Why me? Have you ever asked that question? I have, more times than I care to admit.

There have been times in my life where it appeared nothing was going right for me. There was much hurt, disappointment and trauma throughout the years. In some of my darkest times I would ask God, "Why me?" "Why are things in my life this way?" The Bible tells us in Psalms 34:19, "Many are the afflictions of the righteous…" This does not sound like good news, I know, but it goes on to say "… but the Lord delivers him out of them all." The truth is, being saved does not exempt you from hardships, heartbreaks or disappointment. The difference is that the believer knows that God will rescue them and heal them from all hurt.

In the Old Testament people would wear ashes as a symbol of grief or sorrow. God said to Israel, and He says to us today, "Give me your ashes. I will crown your head with beauty instead." Give all your burdens, despair, disappointments, hurt and anguish to God. Trust Him that even the pain serves a purpose and will work out for your good. In exchange, He will give you peace, joy and love.

Say this: God, I give my life to you. I lay all my burdens, hurt and pain at your feet. I exchange it all for your strength, joy, peace and love.

DAY 14

RELEASE. LET GO.

"Forget the former things; do not dwell on the past. See, I am doing a new thing! Now spring up; do you not perceive it? I am making a way in the wilderness and streams in the wasteland."

Isaiah 43:1-19 NIV

When we make the decision to follow Christ, not only are we saved and set free from the bondage of sin, but God takes the old nature and replaces it with a new nature. We become "reborn". God wants to take all the old and make it new. We, however, sometimes find it difficult to release the old and trust God with the new.

"Getting over a painful experience is much like crossing monkey bars. You have to let go at some point in order to move forward". C. S. Lewis

Letting go of the past is not easy but very necessary. If we want to live a life of joy and peace we must let go of the past hurts. We do this by believing, trusting and allowing God to heal us. He is more than willing and able to do so. We must be willing to do our part, which is turning all our pain over to Him and leaving it with Him. Release the old and receive new life in Jesus Christ.

Pray this: God, today I make the decision to release all the hurt, pain, trauma and disappointments to you. I believe that you have healed me. I will no longer dwell on my past, but I will live in the present and embrace the future.